Hermeticism Simplified:
A Beginner's Guide to the Key Principles and Practices

By Louis Sefer
Copyright © 2023

Terms and Conditions
LEGAL NOTICE

Table of Contents

Preface

Hermeticism is a spiritual tradition that has captured the imagination and inspired the practices of individuals for centuries. With roots tracing back to ancient Egypt, Hermeticism is a tradition that has evolved and adapted over time, incorporating a diverse array of teachings and practices that are designed to support personal transformation and spiritual development.

In this book, we will explore the key principles and practices of Hermeticism, as well as its influence on literature, art, science, and psychology. Through an exploration of the Hermetic Corpus and other primary sources, as well as the insights of modern scholars and practitioners, we will seek to gain a deeper understanding of this rich and multifaceted tradition.

Whether you are a seasoned practitioner of Hermeticism or are simply curious about this fascinating tradition, we hope that this book will provide a valuable resource for your journey of exploration and understanding.

Introduction to Hermeticism

Hermeticism is a philosophical and religious tradition that has its roots in ancient Egypt and the teachings of Hermes Trismegistus, a figure who was revered by the ancient Egyptians as a divine messenger and source of revealed wisdom. The Hermetic Corpus, a collection of texts attributed to Hermes Trismegistus, contains ideas and practices that focus on understanding the nature of the universe and achieving spiritual enlightenment.

At its core, Hermeticism emphasizes the idea that there is a unity between the physical and spiritual worlds, and that it is possible for humans to gain understanding and knowledge of the divine through personal experience and individual contemplation. This holistic worldview has made Hermeticism a popular spiritual tradition throughout history, influencing various philosophical and religious systems and continuing to attract followers in the modern era.

The history of Hermeticism is complex and multifaceted, with roots that can be traced back to ancient Egyptian, Greek, and other cultures. In the centuries following the rise of Christianity, Hermeticism experienced a resurgence in Europe, and has continued to evolve and adapt to new cultural and philosophical contexts.

Today, Hermeticism is a diverse and multifaceted spiritual tradition that offers a wealth of teachings and practices for individuals seeking greater understanding and enlightenment. In the following chapters, we will delve deeper into the history, philosophy, and practices of Hermeticism, exploring the key concepts and ideas that form the foundation of this enduring and influential tradition.

The Teachings of Hermes Trismegistus

At the heart of the Hermetic tradition are the teachings of Hermes Trismegistus, a figure who is revered as the source of revealed wisdom and the patron of alchemy and other esoteric arts. The Hermetic Corpus, a collection of texts attributed to Hermes Trismegistus, contains a wide range of philosophical, spiritual, and practical teachings that form the foundation of Hermeticism.

One of the key ideas in the Hermetic Corpus is the concept of the unity of the physical and spiritual worlds. According to Hermetic teachings, the material world is a manifestation of the divine, and it is possible for humans to gain understanding and knowledge of the divine through personal experience and contemplation. This idea is reflected in the famous Hermetic axiom, "As above, so below," which suggests that the microcosm of the individual mirrors the macrocosm of the universe.

Another important teaching of Hermes Trismegistus is the concept of the "Divine Spark," or the idea that every individual contains a divine essence within them. This Divine Spark is seen as the source of one's true potential and is believed to be the key to achieving spiritual enlightenment.

Other key concepts in the Hermetic Corpus include the Law of Correspondence, the concept of the Great Work, and the idea of transmutation. The Law of Correspondence states that there is a correspondence or connection between the physical and spiritual realms, and that the same principles apply to both. The concept of the Great Work refers to the process of personal transformation and spiritual development that is central to Hermeticism. Finally, the idea of transmutation suggests that it is possible to transform oneself and one's circumstances through spiritual practice and the attainment of higher understanding.

These are just a few of the many teachings and ideas that can be found in the Hermetic Corpus. In the following chapters, we will explore these and other concepts in greater depth, examining their significance and relevance to the Hermetic tradition.

The Core Hermetic Principles: Understanding the Fundamentals of the Tradition

The Hermetic principles are a set of spiritual and philosophical teachings that were first recorded in ancient Egypt and later developed by the Hermetic tradition. These principles are often associated with the ancient Egyptian god Thoth, also known as Hermes Trismegistus, from whom the tradition takes its name.

Here are the seven core Hermetic principles:

1. The Principle of Mentalism: The idea that all things in the universe are manifestations of the mind or consciousness.

2. The Principle of Correspondence: The idea that there is a correspondence or connection between different levels of existence, such as the correspondence between the microcosm and macrocosm.

3. The Principle of Vibration: The idea that all things in the universe are in a constant state of vibration or oscillation.

4. The Principle of Polarity: The idea that all things in the universe have opposite or complementary aspects, and that these are interconnected.

5. The Principle of Rhythm: The idea that all things in the universe are subject to cycles or rhythms.

6. The Principle of Cause and Effect: The idea that for every action, there is a corresponding effect.

7. The Principle of Gender: The idea that all things in the universe possess both masculine and feminine qualities, and that these qualities are interconnected.

It is important to note that the principles of Hermeticism is not only meant to be understood intellectually, but they need to be internalized and practiced.

The Unity of the Physical and Spiritual Worlds

One of the central ideas of Hermeticism is the concept of the unity of the physical and spiritual worlds. According to Hermetic teachings, the material world is not separate from the spiritual realm, but rather a manifestation of the divine. This belief is reflected in the famous Hermetic axiom, "As above, so below," which suggests that the microcosm of the individual mirrors the macrocosm of the universe.

This belief in the unity of the physical and spiritual worlds has important implications for the way that Hermeticism views the nature of reality and the path to spiritual enlightenment. Instead of seeing the material world as an obstacle or distraction, Hermeticism regards the physical world as a valuable source of knowledge and understanding. By studying the natural world and our own experiences, we can gain insights into the nature of the divine and our own place in the universe.

The unity of the physical and spiritual worlds also implies that spiritual growth and personal transformation are not separate from the everyday aspects of our lives. According to Hermeticism, the path to enlightenment is not something that can be pursued in isolation, but rather involves integrating spiritual practices and insights into all aspects of our lives.

In this way, the idea of the unity of the physical and spiritual worlds is central to the holistic worldview of Hermeticism, which sees the individual and the universe as interconnected and inseparable. In the following chapters, we will explore the implications of this idea and how it shapes the practices and goals of Hermeticism.

The Nature of the Universe

Hermeticism is a tradition that seeks to understand the nature of the universe and our place within it. According to Hermetic teachings, the universe is a manifestation of the divine, and it is possible for humans to gain knowledge and understanding of the divine through personal experience and contemplation.

One way that Hermeticism approaches the question of the nature of the universe is through the concept of correspondences. The Law of Correspondence, which is a key idea in the Hermetic Corpus, states that there is a connection or correspondence between the physical and spiritual realms, and that the same principles apply to both. This idea suggests that by studying the natural world and our own experiences, we can gain insights into the nature of the divine and the spiritual realm.

Another way that Hermeticism views the nature of the universe is through the concept of the Great Work. The Great Work refers to the process of personal transformation and spiritual development that is central to Hermeticism. This process involves the individual striving to align themselves with the divine and to achieve a state of spiritual enlightenment.

In addition to these ideas, the Hermetic Corpus contains a wealth of teachings and practices related to the nature of the universe and the path to spiritual enlightenment. In the following chapters, we will explore these teachings and practices in greater depth, examining how they shape the understanding of the universe and the goals of Hermeticism.

The Concept of the Divine

The concept of the divine is central to the Hermetic tradition and is fundamental to the understanding of the universe and the path to spiritual enlightenment. According to Hermeticism, the divine is the ultimate source of all that exists and is the ultimate goal of the spiritual journey.

Hermeticism offers a variety of perspectives on the nature of the divine, and different teachings within the tradition may emphasize different aspects of the divine. However, one common theme is the idea that the divine is the ultimate source of wisdom and understanding, and that it is possible for humans to gain knowledge and insight into the divine through personal experience and contemplation.

Another important aspect of the divine in Hermeticism is the idea that the divine is immanent, or present within all things. This belief suggests that the divine is not separate from the material world, but rather is present within it and can be accessed through spiritual practices and personal experience.

The concept of the divine also plays a central role in the concept of the Great Work, which is the process of personal transformation and spiritual development that is central to Hermeticism. The Great Work is seen as a journey towards aligning oneself with the divine and achieving a state of spiritual enlightenment.

In the following chapters, we will explore the concept of the divine in greater depth, examining the various ways in which it is understood and experienced within the Hermetic tradition.

The Hermetic Concept of the Self

In Hermeticism, the concept of the self is closely tied to the idea of the Divine Spark, which is seen as the source of an individual's true potential and the key to achieving spiritual enlightenment.

According to Hermetic teachings, the Divine Spark is present within every individual and it is the task of the individual to cultivate and nurture this essence in order to reach their full potential.

The process of cultivating the Divine Spark and achieving spiritual enlightenment is known as the Great Work, which is a central concept in Hermeticism. The Great Work involves the individual striving to align themselves with the divine and to achieve a state of spiritual enlightenment.

One of the key aspects of the Great Work is the process of self-discovery and self-exploration. In order to cultivate the Divine Spark and achieve spiritual enlightenment, individuals must delve into their own inner selves and gain a deeper understanding of their own thoughts, feelings, and motivations.

This process of self-exploration can be facilitated through a variety of practices and techniques, including meditation, journaling, and the use of symbolism.

By engaging in these practices and exploring the inner landscape of their own minds, individuals can gain insights into their own nature and their place in the universe.

Hermeticism and the Concept of Reincarnation

The concept of reincarnation, or the belief that the soul is reborn into a new body after death, is a central belief in many spiritual traditions, including Hermeticism. In the Hermetic tradition, reincarnation is seen as an integral part of the spiritual journey and is believed to be a means by which the soul can progress and evolve.

According to Hermetic teachings, the process of reincarnation is governed by the law of karma, which states that the actions and choices of an individual in one life will determine the circumstances of their next life. This belief suggests that the soul is continually reborn into new bodies in order to learn and grow, and that the ultimate goal of the soul is to achieve spiritual enlightenment and liberation from the cycle of reincarnation.

The concept of reincarnation is closely tied to the idea of the Great Work, which is the process of personal transformation and spiritual development that is central to Hermeticism. The Great Work involves the individual striving to align themselves with the divine and to achieve a state of spiritual enlightenment, and it is believed that this process can be facilitated through the process of reincarnation.

In the Hermetic tradition, the concept of reincarnation is seen as a means of understanding the nature of the self and the universe, and it is often explored through practices such as meditation and astral projection, which are believed to allow the individual to access past lives and gain insights into their own spiritual journey.

Hermeticism and the Quest for Meaning

One of the key themes of Hermeticism is the idea that it is possible for individuals to gain understanding and meaning in their lives through personal experience and contemplation. According to Hermetic teachings, the path to enlightenment is a deeply personal journey that involves the cultivation of the Divine Spark within oneself and the alignment with the divine.

The pursuit of understanding and meaning is central to the concept of the Great Work, which is the process of personal transformation and spiritual development that is central to Hermeticism. The Great Work involves the individual striving to achieve a state of spiritual enlightenment and to understand their place in the universe.

Hermeticism offers a range of teachings and practices that can help individuals on their journey towards enlightenment, including meditation, ritual, and the study of the Hermetic Corpus. These practices are designed to help individuals connect with the divine and gain insights into the nature of the universe and their own place within it.

In addition to providing a path towards spiritual enlightenment, the teachings and practices of Hermeticism can also offer guidance and insight for individuals seeking meaning and purpose in their everyday lives. By integrating the principles and practices of Hermeticism into their daily lives, individuals can find greater understanding and fulfillment in their relationships, careers, and other aspects of their lives.

In upcoming chapters, we will explore the ways in which Hermeticism can offer guidance and support for individuals seeking meaning and understanding in their lives, and how the tradition can provide a framework for personal growth and development.

The Role of the Divine Feminine in Hermeticism

In many spiritual traditions, the divine is often depicted as male, with the feminine being seen as secondary or inferior. However, in the Hermetic tradition, the divine feminine plays a central and revered role.

One of the key figures in the Hermetic tradition who embodies the divine feminine is Isis, the ancient Egyptian goddess of fertility, motherhood, and death. Isis is often depicted as a powerful and wise figure, and she is revered as a patroness of magic and the occult.

Another important figure in the Hermetic tradition who represents the divine feminine is Sophia, the personification of wisdom in the Gnostic tradition. Sophia is often depicted as a feminine figure and is revered as a source of knowledge and understanding.

In the Hermetic tradition, the divine feminine is seen as a source of creativity, wisdom, and spiritual power. By recognizing and honoring the divine feminine, individuals can tap into their own inner wisdom and creativity and gain a deeper understanding of the nature of the universe.

In the Hermetic Corpus, the divine feminine is often depicted as the anima mundi, or the soul of the world. This concept suggests that the divine feminine is present within all things and is the source of life and creativity. By recognizing and honoring the divine feminine, individuals can connect with the soul of the world and gain a deeper understanding of their own place within it.

The Role of the Individual in Hermeticism

In Hermeticism, the individual plays a central role in the process of spiritual growth and enlightenment. According to Hermetic teachings, it is through personal experience and individual contemplation that we can gain understanding and knowledge of the divine.

One of the key concepts in this regard is the idea of the Divine Spark, which is seen as the source of an individual's true potential and the key to achieving spiritual enlightenment. The Divine Spark is believed to be present within every individual, and it is the task of the individual to cultivate and nurture this essence in order to reach their full potential.

The process of cultivating the Divine Spark and achieving spiritual enlightenment is known as the Great Work. The Great Work is a central concept in Hermeticism and refers to the process of personal transformation and spiritual development. It involves the individual striving to align themselves with the divine and to achieve a state of spiritual enlightenment.

The Great Work is a deeply personal and individual process, and it is up to each individual to determine their own path and goals. However, Hermeticism does offer a range of teachings and practices that can help individuals on their journey towards enlightenment, including meditation, ritual, and the study of the Hermetic Corpus.

In the following chapters, we will explore the role of the individual in Hermeticism in greater depth, examining the various ways in which individuals can engage with the tradition and pursue the Great Work.

The Role of Community in Hermeticism

In many spiritual traditions, the concept of community plays a central role, with individuals coming together to support each other on their spiritual journeys and to explore and practice their beliefs. This is also true of the Hermetic tradition, which has a long history of individuals coming together to study, practice, and share their understanding of the teachings and practices of the tradition.

One way in which community is important in the Hermetic tradition is through the use of spiritual groups or organizations. These groups provide a forum for individuals to come together to study and practice Hermeticism, and they often offer a range of resources and support for those interested in the tradition.

In addition to formal groups, community is also important in the Hermetic tradition through the formation of informal networks and relationships. These relationships can provide a sense of connection and support for individuals on their spiritual journey, and they can be an important source of guidance and inspiration.

Overall, the concept of community is central to the Hermetic tradition, with individuals coming together to support and inspire each other on their journey towards spiritual enlightenment. By building and participating in a supportive community, individuals can find greater meaning and fulfillment in their spiritual practice.

The Role of Ritual and Magic in Hermeticism

Ritual and magic play an important role in the Hermetic tradition, serving as tools for personal transformation and spiritual development. According to Hermeticism, ritual and magic are means of accessing and interacting with the divine and can be used to achieve specific goals or to bring about personal transformation.

One of the key practices in Hermeticism is the use of ritual, which involves the performance of specific actions or ceremonies in order to invoke or honor the divine. These rituals can take a variety of forms, including prayer, meditation, chanting, and the use of symbolic objects or gestures.

Magic, as it is understood in the Hermetic tradition, is the use of ritual and other techniques to bring about specific outcomes or to achieve certain goals. This can involve the use of spells, incantations, and other practices that are believed to harness the power of the divine or the natural world.

The use of ritual and magic in Hermeticism is closely tied to the idea of the Great Work, which is the process of personal transformation and spiritual development that is central to the tradition. Ritual and magic are seen as tools that can help individuals on their journey towards enlightenment, allowing them to access and interact with the divine in a meaningful way.

In the following chapters, we will explore the role of ritual and magic in Hermeticism in greater depth, examining the various practices and techniques that are used within the tradition.

Hermeticism and the Use of Symbolism

Symbolism plays a central role in the Hermetic tradition, serving as a means of expressing and exploring spiritual concepts and ideas. In Hermeticism, symbols are seen as vehicles for transmitting knowledge and understanding, and they are often used in a variety of contexts, including ritual, art, and literature.

One of the key symbols in Hermeticism is the caduceus, which is a staff entwined by two serpents. The caduceus is often associated with Hermes Trismegistus, the patron of alchemy and other esoteric arts, and it is believed to represent the balance between the material and spiritual realms.

Another important symbol in Hermeticism is the pentagram, which is a five-pointed star that is often used to represent the four elements (earth, air, fire, and water) and the spirit. The pentagram is often used in Hermetic rituals and is believed to symbolize the integration of the physical and spiritual aspects of the individual.

Other symbols that are commonly used in Hermeticism include the ouroboros, which is a serpent or dragon that is depicted as swallowing its own tail, and the Tree of Life, which is a symbol that represents the interconnectedness of all things.

In the Hermetic tradition, symbols are seen as powerful tools for understanding and exploring spiritual concepts and ideas, and they are often used as a means of connecting with the divine and gaining insights into the nature of the universe.

The Relationship Between Hermeticism and Other Spiritual Traditions

Hermeticism has a long and complex history, and its teachings and practices have been influenced by a variety of philosophical and spiritual traditions. At the same time, Hermeticism has also had a significant impact on other spiritual systems, and its ideas and practices can be found in a range of religious and philosophical contexts.

One tradition with which Hermeticism has had a close relationship is alchemy. Alchemy is a spiritual and philosophical tradition that seeks to understand the nature of the universe and to achieve spiritual enlightenment through the transmutation of matter. The Hermetic Corpus, which is a key text in the Hermetic tradition, contains a wealth of teachings and practices related to alchemy, and many alchemical texts make reference to Hermetic ideas and concepts.

Another tradition with which Hermeticism has had a close relationship is Kabbalah, a Jewish mystical tradition that seeks to understand the nature of God and the universe. Hermeticism and Kabbalah share many common themes and ideas, and it is believed that some of the teachings of Hermes Trismegistus may have influenced the development of Kabbalah.

Hermeticism has also had a significant influence on various modern spiritual and philosophical movements, including the New Age movement and various esoteric schools of thought. These movements have adopted and adapted many Hermetic ideas and practices, often incorporating them into a broader spiritual worldview.

In the following chapters, we will explore the relationship between Hermeticism and other spiritual traditions in greater depth, examining the ways in which these traditions have influenced and been influenced by each other.

The Connection Between Hermeticism and Psychology

In recent times, there has been a growing recognition of the connection between Hermeticism and psychology, with many psychologists and other mental health professionals exploring the potential benefits of incorporating Hermetic principles and practices into their work.

One area where there has been particular interest is the use of Hermetic principles and practices in the treatment of psychological disorders. For example, some therapists have found that incorporating meditation and other Hermetic practices into their treatment plans can be effective in helping clients to manage stress, reduce anxiety, and improve overall well-being.

Another area where there has been interest is the use of Hermetic principles and practices in personal growth and development. Many individuals have found that engaging with Hermetic teachings and practices can be a powerful tool for personal transformation and spiritual development.

In addition to these applications, there is also a growing body of research exploring the psychological and neurophysiological effects of Hermetic practices such as meditation. This research suggests that these practices can have a variety of positive effects on the brain and behavior, including improved cognitive functioning, reduced stress and anxiety, and improved overall well-being.

Overall, the connection between Hermeticism and psychology highlights the potential benefits of incorporating spiritual practices into our lives and the ways in which they can support personal growth and well-being.

Hermeticism and Science: Bridging the Divide

The relationship between Hermeticism and science has often been seen as an either/or proposition, with these two ways of understanding the world being viewed as mutually exclusive. However, in recent years, there has been a growing recognition that Hermeticism and science can actually complement and inform each other, bridging the divide between these seemingly disparate fields.

One way in which Hermeticism and science intersect is through the study of physics. Some physicists and philosophers have explored the ways in which Hermetic concepts, such as the idea of the interconnectedness of all things, can be seen as reflecting principles of quantum physics. This suggests that Hermeticism and science may be more closely aligned than previously thought.

In addition to this overlap in the realm of physics, there is also growing evidence of the positive effects that Hermetic practices, such as meditation, can have on the brain and body. Research has shown that meditation can reduce stress and anxiety, improve cognitive functioning, and enhance overall well-being. These scientifically measurable effects provide further evidence of the ways in which Hermeticism and science can inform and enrich each other.

Overall, the relationship between Hermeticism and science highlights the potential benefits of incorporating spiritual practices and perspectives into our understanding of the world, and the ways in which these approaches can work together to create a more holistic and nuanced understanding of reality.

.

The Modern Revival of Hermeticism

Despite its ancient origins, Hermeticism has experienced a resurgence in popularity in recent times, with many individuals and groups seeking to rediscover and explore its teachings and practices. This modern revival of Hermeticism has been driven by a variety of factors, including a renewed interest in ancient spiritual traditions and a search for alternative spiritual paths.

One of the key figures in the modern revival of Hermeticism is Aleister Crowley, a British occultist and ceremonial magician who was heavily influenced by the Hermetic Corpus and other esoteric traditions. Crowley's writings and teachings helped to spread interest in Hermeticism and other esoteric traditions, and he is still regarded as an important figure in contemporary esotericism.

In addition to Crowley, there have been numerous other figures and organizations that have contributed to the modern revival of Hermeticism. These include the Golden Dawn, a secret society that was influential in the late 19th and early 20th centuries, and various contemporary esoteric groups that draw on Hermetic teachings and practices.

The modern revival of Hermeticism has also been fueled by the growth of the New Age movement, which has embraced a variety of spiritual and philosophical traditions, including Hermeticism. As a result, many of the teachings and practices of Hermeticism can be found in contemporary New Age literature and spiritual practices.

In the following chapters, we will explore the modern revival of Hermeticism in greater depth, examining the various factors that have contributed to its resurgence and the ways in which it has adapted and evolved in contemporary contexts.

The Influence of Hermeticism on Literature and Art

Throughout its long history, Hermeticism has had a significant influence on literature and art, with many writers, artists, and intellectuals being inspired by the tradition's teachings and practices. This influence can be seen in a variety of contexts, from literature and poetry to visual art, music, and film.

One of the key figures in the history of literature and art who was heavily influenced by Hermeticism was the poet and artist William Blake. Blake was deeply interested in Hermetic teachings and incorporated many Hermetic themes and symbols into his work, including the concept of the Divine Spark and the idea of the Great Work.

Another writer who was influenced by Hermeticism was the poet and mystic William Butler Yeats. Yeats was a member of the Golden Dawn, a secret society that was influenced by Hermeticism and other esoteric traditions, and his poetry and prose often explores themes of personal transformation and spiritual development that are central to Hermeticism.

In more recent times, Hermeticism has also had an influence on contemporary literature and art. For example, the poet and writer Allen Ginsberg was influenced by Hermetic teachings and incorporated many Hermetic themes and symbols into his work.

Overall, the influence of Hermeticism on literature and art highlights the enduring appeal and relevance of the tradition's teachings and practices, and the ways in which they have inspired and influenced creative expression across time and culture.

Contemporary Expressions of Hermeticism

Despite its ancient roots, Hermeticism continues to be a vibrant and relevant tradition in the modern world, with many individuals exploring and practicing its teachings and practices. There are a variety of ways in which Hermeticism is expressed in the contemporary world, including through formal organizations, spiritual groups, and individual practice.

One way in which Hermeticism is expressed in the modern world is through the use of online resources and communities. Many websites and online groups offer information and support for individuals interested in exploring the Hermetic tradition, and these resources can be a valuable source of information and connection for those seeking to learn more about the tradition.

In addition to online resources, there are also a variety of spiritual groups and organizations that offer Hermetic teachings and practices in a more traditional setting. These groups can provide a sense of community and connection for individuals interested in exploring the tradition, and they often offer a range of resources and support for those seeking to deepen their understanding and practice.

Overall, the contemporary expression of Hermeticism highlights the enduring relevance and appeal of the tradition, and the ways in which it continues to inspire and guide individuals in the modern world.

Hermetic Practices for Personal Transformation

One of the key goals of Hermeticism is personal transformation and spiritual development, and the tradition offers a range of practices and techniques that are designed to support this process. These practices can be used to help individuals connect with the divine, gain insights into their own nature, and achieve a state of spiritual enlightenment.

One of the primary practices in Hermeticism is meditation, which is seen as a means of accessing the innermost depths of the self and gaining insight into the nature of the universe. There are many different types of meditation that are used in the Hermetic tradition, including mindfulness meditation, breath meditation, and mantra meditation.

Another important practice in Hermeticism is the use of ritual, which involves the performance of specific actions or ceremonies in order to invoke or honor the divine. These rituals can take a variety of forms, including prayer, chanting, and the use of symbolic objects or gestures.

In addition to meditation and ritual, other practices that are commonly used in Hermeticism include the study of the Hermetic Corpus and other esoteric texts, the use of astrology and other divination techniques, and the practice of alchemy.

By engaging in these practices, individuals can gain a deeper understanding of their own nature and their place in the universe and can work towards achieving a state of spiritual enlightenment and personal transformation.

A Practical Guide to Integrating Ancient Wisdom into Modern Life

There are several ways in which you can actively apply the Hermetic principles in your life. Here are a few examples:

1. The Principle of Mentalism: To actively apply this principle, you can practice mindfulness and meditation, to become more aware of the thoughts and emotions that influence your actions and decisions. You can also practice visualization and affirmation, to manifest your desired reality.

2. The Principle of Correspondence: To actively apply this principle, you can study the principles of astrology, numerology, and tarot, to understand the correspondences between the different levels of existence. You can also study the symbolism of different cultures, to gain a deeper understanding of the correspondences between the microcosm and macrocosm.

3. The Principle of Vibration: To actively apply this principle, you can practice yoga and other forms of movement, to attune yourself to the vibrations of your body. You can also study the principles of sound and music, to understand the vibrations of sound and the way they can be used to heal and transform.

4. The Principle of Polarity: To actively apply this principle, you can practice the art of balance, to understand and integrate the polarities within yourself and in the world. You can also practice the art of reconciliation, to understand how polarities can be reconciled and how to use them to create harmony.

5. The Principle of Rhythm: To actively apply this principle, you can practice the art of timing, to attune yourself to the rhythms of nature and the universe. You can also practice the art of cyclical thinking, to understand how to live in harmony with the rhythms of life.

6. The Principle of Cause and Effect: To actively apply this principle, you can practice the art of responsibility, to understand and take responsibility for the causes and effects of your actions.

7. The Principle of Gender: To actively apply this principle, you can practice the art of integration, to understand and integrate the masculine and feminine aspects of your psyche.

It is important to note that these are just examples, and the practice of Hermeticism is not limited to these, there are many other ways to apply the principles in daily life, and it can also be different for each person depending on their circumstances and understanding.

Conclusion

Throughout its long history, the Hermetic tradition has provided a rich source of teachings and practices for personal transformation and spiritual development. Its emphasis on the individual's quest for enlightenment and its recognition of the divine within all things have made it a powerful and enduring tradition that continues to inspire and guide individuals in the modern world.

In this book, we have explored the key principles and practices of Hermeticism, including the concept of the Divine Spark, the Great Work, and the use of symbolism and ritual. We have also examined the ways in which Hermeticism has influenced and been influenced by other fields, including psychology, science, and literature and art.

In the final analysis, the enduring appeal of Hermeticism lies in its emphasis on personal growth and spiritual development. By engaging with its teachings and practices, individuals can gain a deeper understanding of their own nature and their place in the universe and can work towards achieving a state of spiritual enlightenment and personal transformation.

About The Author

Louis 'Lou' Sefer is a dedicated occult, spiritual, and metaphysical student. He has studied the teachings of different esoteric, magickal, and mystical schools and practices over the years, as well as hundreds of books on the subjects.

Lou is obsessed with gathering, researching, and assimilation of ancient knowledge in search of the truth. He has an honorary Doctor of Divinity from one institution. He is also an ordained minister. He prefers to remain anonymous.

Author of the Best Seller '*Sacred Secrets of Esoteric Christianity*' and '*Mysteries of the Soul*' both available for sale on Amazon.

Visit www.louissefer.com and join the Esoteric Evolution blog where you can find several articles and resources into esoteric Christianity, Hermeticism and more. You can also access free previews of Lou's books.

Further Reading

Here are some of the most well-known and widely respected texts on the subject of Hermeticism:

1. "The Hermetica: The Lost Wisdom of the Pharaohs" by Timothy Freke and Peter Gandy

2. "The Kybalion: A Study of the Hermetic Philosophy of Ancient Egypt and Greece" by Three Initiates

3. "The Emerald Tablet: An Illustrated Guide to the Timeless Wisdom of Hermes Trismegistus" by Dennis William Hauck

4. "The Hermetic Brotherhood of Luxor: Initiatic and Historical Documents of an Order of Practical Occultism" edited by Joscelyn Godwin

5. "The Divine Pymander of Hermes Mercurius Trismegistus" translated by John Everard

6. "The Hermetic Tradition: Symbols and Teachings of the Royal Art" by Julius Evola

7. "The Hermetica: The Lost Wisdom of the Pharaohs" by Walter Scott

8. "Hermeticism: An Introduction" by Christopher McIntosh

9. "Hermeticism: The History and Practices of a Mystical Tradition" by Chris Marshall

10. "The Hermetic Code in DNA: The Sacred Principles in the Ordering of the Universe" by Laurence Gardner

11. "The Hermetic Museum, Vol. I" edited by Arthur Edward Waite

12. "The Complete Corpus Hermeticum" translated by G.R.S. Mead

13. "The Hermetica: The Lost Wisdom of the Pharaohs" by Brian Copenhaver

14. "The Secret Teachings of All Ages" by Manly P. Hall

15. "Hermeticism: The Essential Writings" edited by Jacob Needleman

Made in United States
Troutdale, OR
01/12/2024

16920646R00030